To Mrs. M Mins

Wow what
I was so excited the very first time I met you.
You have **ALWAYS** displayed good character and an Awesome sweet spirit.
I Love your Style" ☺
I'm taking notes for my future.

Stay Sweet, Stay Awesome. and forever Serving God & his people

Ms. Laura S. R____

4/20/2011

much peace & Love

TRAPPED
IN THE SYSTEM

Ms. Larita S. Rice

authorHOUSE®

AuthorHouse™
1663 Liberty Drive
Bloomington, IN 47403
www.authorhouse.com
Phone: 1-800-839-8640

© 2011 Ms. Larita S. Rice. All rights reserved.

No part of this book may be reproduced, stored in a retrieval system, or transmitted by any means without the written permission of the author.

First published by AuthorHouse 4/7/2011

ISBN: 978-1-4567-4820-3 (e)
ISBN: 978-1-4567-4821-0 (hc)
ISBN: 978-1-4567-4822-7 (sc)

Library of Congress Control Number: 2011904468

Printed in the United States of America

Any people depicted in stock imagery provided by Thinkstock are models, and such images are being used for illustrative purposes only. Certain stock imagery © Thinkstock.

This book is printed on acid-free paper.

Because of the dynamic nature of the Internet, any web addresses or links contained in this book may have changed since publication and may no longer be valid. The views expressed in this work are solely those of the author and do not necessarily reflect the views of the publisher, and the publisher hereby disclaims any responsibility for them.

Table of Contents

Her Story	vii
Acknowledgements	xiii
Prelude	xv
Trapped Introduction	xvii
Chapter 1 Trapped	1
Chapter 2 What to do when everybody's gone	9
Chapter 3 Strength in the face of opposition	15
Chapter 4 Thought Patterns of Life	27
Chapter 5 Opposition From Within	39
Chapter 6 At the Breaking Point	53
Chapter 7 The pain of sacrifice	59
Chapter 8 Living out of the Hand of God	65
Chapter 9 Getting real with Yourself	71
Chapter 10 It's Time to get Connected	79
Chapter 11 Processed for Change	83
Book Resources	93

Her Story

June 8, 1975 God sent forth an angel to walk the Earth with wings that weren't clipped because they weren't developed. An unaware Eagle without a clue what step she should take next, who lived in fear because she was afraid to fly, and was bound because it was many years before she left the nest because she was always afraid to take risks, she was afraid to hear the opinions of others. An Eagle that was forced to learn how to fly on her own, an eagle that didn't receive the proper support from her family to continue to fly.

As a child she often times found herself talking to her imaginary daughter Tika and imaginary husband Laundromat to erase the loneliness she felt, to discard her feelings of abandonment, neglect, and low-self esteem. The same child that took on a major responsibility of being a prayer warrior for her family was the same child who smiled through her pain. The same child that found herself molested is the same child that found herself standing in the gap for her love ones when they couldn't stand at all. She was the same child that would go days, weeks, or maybe a month or so without seeing her father is the same woman who accepted her father again as an adult.

This woman is indeed an angelic Eagle! An Eagle is a very large bird that awaits for the next storm because it has an opportunity to soar to its highest heights. An Eagle uses the pressures of the winds, and the updrafts to press against its wings so it can continue moving upward and towards its next destination for such a time as this.

The same woman who realized that there was a God after being in an abusive relationship for about four years suffering from a chair thrown at her head repeatedly and a foot print on the side of her head while the other side lay on the glass attacked concrete. After being an alcoholic since middle school, a drug-dealer, and a victim of rape is the same woman who prayed and fought for her family spiritual transformation while managing to be the first high school graduate in her family.

This great woman of faith overcame every obstacle that was meant to bring her down, knock the Eagle out the sky, and stop her from reaching the heights of glory. The same woman who escaped every trap the devil set for her and even the holes she had dug herself decided not to let her life be destroyed, her dreams be unrealistic, and aspirations to fall by the waste side. After being in a household with alcoholics, drug addicts and verbal abusers she made a step to move out naturally to prepare herself for God's spiritual move. With her one year old child she continued to press toward the mark and pray on through her problems. This woman of God received a word from God in the year of 1997 telling her to get her house in order. She answered to God and at that point she made a conscious decision to never turn back.

She worked at a transitional living center <u>Call for HELP</u>, helping teenagers with the same untold story as hers. She took these teenagers to church faithfully, connected with them, bonded with them as she did with her own child. Soon she was to be terminated from her job not understanding why because she worked with the power of God reigning. From then on having a stable job seemed hard to accomplish. Volunteering and working to fulfill the purpose of God often times left her drained in every way possible. She continued to be faithful to God attending church everyday of the week even that became draining for her; especially since no one at the church seem to help her, but only talk about her for numerous reasons one for her having a child out of wedlock.

After so many years of being apart of an unhealthy ministry she made a transition to higher heights and deeper depths. Still she remained a faithful attendant of church. She found herself being misused for her gifts, talents, money, and time to put on a show for people and not for ministry. After having another child out of wedlock she hid herself from the world, and masked her inner being because of the embarrassment she felt and even dropped out of college.

With me being a child of this amazing woman of God I know exactly how the spiritual and emotional healing transformation process takes place. My mother possesses every characteristic of an Eagle because she teaches and trains her children in away they won't stray way from her teachings when they're old. An Eagle doesn't eat meat that it doesn't kill and my mother realizes that she has to go out, and come forth to makes things happen. Also an Eagle can see great distances and she realizes that without a vision the people perish and that you need divine guidance to move forward.

She continued to allow God to move on her behalf and in the year of 2007 she became the founder of the organization *Women of Excellence Midwest*. An organization that is used to bring empowerment to battered, bruised, abused, and rejected women to remind them there is hope in every situation. To provide a center for crisis intervention that gives resources to help these women without them being judged. She continues to allow God to direct her path while she recently returned back to college for criminal justice to bring God into the federal systems so that some things can be "untrapped." Evangelist Larita Rice, my mother is a woman of God, prayer warrior, soldier for the Lord, spiritual warfare fighter, victor from rape and molestation, ex alcoholic and gang-banger remains steadfast and unmovable always abounding in the work of the Lord reminding others that there work isn't in vain.

Acknowledgements

I would first like to thank God for granting me the grace, courage and strength to produce this book. I would like to thank my daughters Canesha and Camille for always praying for me and speaking life into my spirit. Love ya babes for believing in mommy. I would like to thank my mom and dad Ned and Carolyn whom God allowed to be conduits for my arrival.

To my uncles and aunts whom I love very much may the joy of the Lord be your strength. To my brother Deontae who I am waiting on your new release to hit the press I know it's going to shake hell up. Come forth Man of God come forth. To my wonderful Pastors whom God has blessed me with Elder Kenneth and Prophetess Tonya Stewart and my World Overcomer's Christian Center Fellowship Family, I couldn't have been thrust into my destiny without your love, compassion, vision to see, tenacity to pray the hell out of my life and the boldness to confront the enemy face to face.

To Mildred Eastern- Scott thank you for using

spiritual warfare tactics to disrupt the plans of the enemy for my life through your healing and deliverance ministry. To Elder Leo Mullins despite criticism and ill judgments you have continued to allow God to lead you and support my endeavors Love Ya. To all of those who prayed for me, supported me with my endeavors, listened to my crying and screaming while carrying this baby especially T-Ressa May God's face forever shine upon you. Thank you to my editor in chief Prophetess Val Hopson. A special acknowledgement to my Grandmother Mrs. Martha Rebecca Rice I miss you so much but I know you are on the other side of glory still believing in me and to Pastor Shirley Deavens who is waiting in the sky I bless God for you speaking to all the hindrances in my life and having ministry soil that was so fertile that when anything that was dead touched it, it came to life.

Blessings and Peace
Larita S. Rice

Prelude

Trapped- A confining or undesirable circumstance from which escape or relief is difficult: *fell into poverty's trap.*

It Seems out of Control!!!!

Have you ever just sat down and thought about things that was so out of control. Things that make you go OOOOOOO-AAAAHHHH, well you get it. It makes you scream. It could be things in your life or someone you know. Well let's take a moment to think about some of these things. I know you are tired of thinking about it but Just do it! You did it when **Nike** told you. The point is you don't like thinking about those things because you feel trapped. Feeling trapped has a way of making you feel suffocated when there is no plastic or pillow over your face. It makes you feel helpless which causes your momentum to be drained leaving your body limp and lifeless. According to the American Heritage Dictionary it defines Trapped as A confining or undesirable circumstance from which escape or relief is difficult.

Trapped Introduction

Oftentimes in life we are faced with many challenges. Life has a way of tossing you and turning you. It sometimes shake you up so bad you don't know what the next move should be. In today's society things are constantly changing, with the increase in things from childcare to gasoline one must have a serious plan or a definite anchor in the Lord that is.

Because many are experiencing lack that have never dealt with it before, it is forcing them to develop fears and phobias. This is forced to be viewed unavoidable especially with the news media constantly painting the picture that we are in recession. One of the things that I have come to know is that the one book that has brought so much controversy is true. Yea you know what I am talking about the Bible, the Holy Bible that is. It has been plainly written by the inspiration of the Holy Spirit orchestrated by God and it says even a fool can't error. It describes a gang of events, illustrations and the like to help us as Christians be able to get from point A to Point Z. It has already declared that the day of famine will come, Earthquakes in divers places will come, wars and rumors of wars will come but the end is not yet. It has stated that we will pray for peace and destruction will come.

We are not to be discouraged by things that we see. The Apostle Paul describes this in the book of 2 Corinthians 4:17-18. For our light affliction, which is but for a moment, worketh for us a far more exceeding and eternal weight of glory; While we look not at the things which are seen, but at the things which are not seen: for the things which are seen are temporal; but the things which are not seen are eternal.

We are not to be moved from our firm foundation of God based on what we see but we should remain standing based on what we believe and that is the report of our Lord. God will take care of his people but we must trust him *No Matter What.*

Chapter 1

Trapped

Trapped is a feeling that can bring a lot of anxiety, fears and stagnation. Are these feelings that you can relate to? Well guess what I can too. I know what it feels like to want to progress, you want to conquer, you want to succeed. I remember day after day month after month and year after year wanting my life to change.

I remember sitting on my back porch as a little girl creating my imaginary friends and family. My husband's name was Laundromat and my daughter's name was Tika. I dreamt of what life would be when I grew up. I longed for that perfect family. My father and mother in the house and everything working in harmony, well a dream was all it was. My father was not in the house. It was my mom, my grandma who I called "Gramma" and me. There was not a father figure. As time went on my uncle came and lived with us. Yeah you're probably thinking your uncle was a male who could exemplify a father figure. Well that holds some truth but it was not a reality at least not in my house. My uncle had no success stories of what a father should be.

Although my two uncle's and my mom were born under holy matrimony their up bringing was similar to mine a broken disenfranchised home that was fostered by love accompanied with hurt, anger, bitterness, resentfulness and unforgiveness all seeds that the enemy intended to be planted in my life and eventually it begin to grow in me.

At about three years old I was en-trusted into the hands of my neighbors. While there I began to get introduced to some things that later on would cause me to have a self-complex and look at myself as a failure.

I began to be molested and I was encouraged to fondle his grown body parts. This continued for a while. If this weren't enough, another grown neighbor and I would get in my uncle's car and fondle around. I still remember the aroma from his body parts.

This continued but later began to cease. Although the activities stopped the thoughts kept rolling and the seeds began to grow.

Around the age of 12, I began to have sex. I later got introduced to drugs alcohol and gang affiliation soon followed. Growing up in the heart of the ghetto has its disadvantages too. I would describe the ghetto as a place that lacks resources, has a lot of crime, broken relationships and disenfranchised neighborhoods. These things either destroy you or make you.

For me, I had thoughts of suicide. Spirits of depression, and verges of losing my mind. I was simply at the breaking point. Sometimes we don't seem to understand the reason why we go through certain things.

We can't seem to grasp the reality that we must travel down the highways and by-ways called trials and tribulation.

Quite often there are times when the road becomes so dark that every time we move we're running into something. Sometimes our thinking becomes so cloudy that we just can't seem to operate with clear thoughts.

The pressure becomes so heavy that we feel pushed to make decisions that become life threatening sending us down the road of destruction. It is right here that we become so dimmed in our spirits. We are so deaf in our ears until we can't even hear God. We become so disconnected that we can't feel or see God anywhere. God where are you we ask? Why do you leave me alone to deal with this?

We can't help but remember the prayers we have prayed and the biblical records of the psalmist David, says in Psalms 31," but I have trusted in thee,O Lord: I said thou art my God. For my life is spent with grief and my years with sighing".

My strength faileth. Have mercy upon me O Lord for I am in trouble: mine eye is consumed with grief yea my soul and my belly we remind the lord that he said he wouldn't put more on us than we can bear sometimes ignoring the fact that some of these things we brought on ourselves. Never the less it is hard for us to escape these feelings of abandonment.

Likewise it was for Jesus. St. Mark 15:34 and at the ninth hour Jesus cried with a loud voice saying Eloi, Eloi lama sabachthani? Which is being interpreted, My God, My God why hast thou forsaken me? If Jesus being the divine son of man, who knew no sin, did no sin, had complete purity inside and out, sent to be the ultimate sacrifice for our sins was filled with anguish we should expect nothing less when we are faced with challenges, obstacles, and transitions.

Abandonment is a natural feeling when we become overwhelmed. It causes us to feel alone and forsaken. Hebrews speaks on this in chapter 4: 14-16 "seeing then that we have a great high priest, that is passed into heavens".

Jesus the Son of God, let us hold fast our profession. For we have not a high priest which cannot be touched with the feeling of our Infirmities, but was in all points tempted as we are yet without sin. Let us therefore come boldly unto the throne of grace that we may obtain mercy and find grace to help in time of need.

Ms. Larita S. Rice

Poem from the heart

Problem after problem trial after trial;
Seeking the blessings of the mercy child.

Lord will you please show me the way;
Because if you don't I'll go astray.

Though the enemy comes to attack your faith;
I can hear the voice of the Lord saying child just wait.

Patience is a virtue and love is the key;
Lord will you please instill these in me.

The daily battles sometimes get hard;
But don't be discouraged the battle is the Lord's.

So my friends don't give up but continue to trust;
For the reward is given to the righteous and the just.

Chapter 2

What to do when everybody's gone

Often times those we love, embrace and support fail to be there for us when we need them that can cause us to feel abandoned. We feel let down, emotionally abused and forsaken. We can't seem to phantom why they would leave us alone over and over again. In our minds we replay everything that we have ever done for them, every encouraging word we spoke to them and all the nights we went without sleep just for them and in return this is what we get a no call no show.

They remind you of all the things they must take care of and how at this moment they just simply don't have time for you. Can I get a witness? Listening to them repeat this over and over again just seems to weaken your very soul doesn't it?

Well my brother or my sister this simply means that you have put too much in another man's basket. Didn't the bible tell you to put not your confidence in man? Didn't it tell you what we do for people we should do it as unto God?

Didn't it tell you that God is our rewarder? Then why are you so distraught because they left you alone. Why are you so disappointed because they walked out or never even showed up? Did you forget that Jesus said lo I am with you always? Didn't he tell you he will never leave you or forsake you?

Well, why are you tripping? I'll tell you why, you have forgotten that God is your rewarder. You have forgotten that God is a present help in your time of trouble. You must program yourself to remember people come and people go.

Some people are assigned to your life for a season and others for a lifetime. But all are assigned for a specific reason. You must seek God to find out the purpose of every relationship that involves you. When people walk out of your life, let them walk. You have to learn to rejoice in what seems to be the biggest hurt ever. You must trust that God has a master plan concerning you. Let them go because that's space made for something or someone else new.

You can not put new wine in old wineskins. Let God do something new in you.

Some people are just space fillers they don't mean you any good. They drain you. They are backstabbers and dream killers. They like living under the auspices of evil. You never learn who your true friends are until a crisis hit. True friends pray with you. True friends pray for you. In times of crisis true friends seek ways to aid the situation. Those that don't have an interest of any kind to assist you use the crisis as a way out of your life.

Don't get mad when they leave rejoice because you discovered who they were before God allowed you to go to your next level.

You see God knows what's best. He is sitting high and looking down at this stage play of life. He never sleeps or slumbers. He knows where every person is located. He knows what role they will ultimately play. God knows if the characters roles will clash. He knows if a part needs to be added or removed. He can see the whole picture. You see he sees the beginning, the middle and the end. Relationships have a way of blind siding us. It causes us to ignore the signs of life.

Don't ignore the signs of life they are there for a reason. Don't pause at a stop sign when you know you are suppose to stop. Don't speed up at a caution light when you know you are suppose to slow down. Ignoring the signs can cause you to miss important information that is critical for your next move.

When everybody's gone that you thought would be there don't worry just remember to put all your trust in God knowing that he has a master plan and he's working it out for you.

The Struggle Is Over

Once I go I'm gone, I'm never coming back;
I will fix my eyes and be determined not to get off track.

This road has been so hard and the journey has been real rough;
But through it all I made it over built up, strong, and tough.

Now it's time to say goodbye, another chapter to it's end;
So now I'll wipe my eyes and give a toast to the New Life I can now begin.

By:Larita Shanta Rice
*an encouraging word

Chapter 3
Strength in the face of opposition

Have you ever been faced with a hard decision? Perhaps you are dealing with a chronic illness and the doctor has said there's no cure. You must first realize that in this very place in your life you need strength in the face of opposition. Sometimes finding strength could be one of the most challenging tasks of all times.

But, remember the word of God has declared in Corinthians that when we are weak; God is strong and his strength is made perfect during our weakness. The trials, tests and oppositions of this life can sometimes knock the wind out of you.

Ms. Larita S. Rice

I remember when I was working diligent and faithful in this ministry and all hell broke loose. I had been involved with someone who was a part of the ministry only to discover he was also involved with others. I was basically at that time considered to be a babe in Christ and didn't respond in the manner of which God required.

I was unlearned and still going through a process of recovery from my past. I didn't hold my tongue during these times; I should have and I didn't rapidly flee temptations. I was hurt and felt betrayed because he denied me, lied on me and painted a picture of me being delusional and crazy.

Many people fled from the congregation and I was blamed for this as well. Because he was a compulsive liar and frequently practiced living multiple lives, carried his bible and put on a great show. People believed him.

This almost destroyed me. I got fed up with church folk and all the jargon that came with it.

I developed a strong I DON'T CARE SPIRIT. I didn't want to do anything in the church and I had lost respect for what was referred to as so called leaders. I had been behind the scenes and I saw the scandal and heard the talk and frankly didn't want to deal with leadership.

The spirit of God began to open my eyes to what would change my life forever. In the midst of having an I DON'T CARE SPIRIT, I said I didn't care if I lived or if I died. I didn't care if I got pregnant or not. Keep in mind I was not married. I DON'T CARE attitude is the worst place in life to be.

I saw myself becoming pregnant but was not in a proper place spiritually to understand. I knew you had to have sex to become pregnant and at the time I was not sexually involved with anyone. I was so zapped spiritually that I didn't realize what the devil was trying to do.

He was planting seeds and instead of me plucking them up (rebuking it) I let them grow. Guess what I got pregnant in 15 minutes or less. It was not pleasurable at all especially because of the sin and condemnation. He lied about the semen. I laid there as though I was a dead woman. I was totally not in tune with my purpose. During this season I thought that my life was over. I discovered that my life was just beginning.

What the devil meant for bad God made it good. I almost became discouraged about talking to the youth. The devil would say to me who's gonna listen to you? What can you tell them? It was during this time I learned who my true friends were.

Those who confessed holy but holy didn't obey Galatians when it said ye that are spiritual are to restore those that are weak lest you fall into the same temptations. They did talk about me.

The ones who I thought would stay left and those who I thought would leave stayed. God showed himself mighty. I endured great persecution. I felt condemned by myself and by people. I was judged and ridiculed. God spoke to me one day and said people don't have a heaven or hell to put you in or the power to get you out of either one of them.

This got me through one of the toughest times of my life and continues to uplift me.

Ms. Larita S. Rice

I considered abortion because the pressure of my surroundings was so great. I wasn't sure if I could stand. The devil was trying to kill me and my child spiritually and physically. My mind was plagued by the enemy. I brought this idea to my child's father and he was shocked because this was outside of my character.

Later the idea grew on him and he thought we should proceed. I want you to know God is good. At this time I had been finding little increments of time to seek God.

My child's father would constantly say let's go to the clinic and at least talk to them. I will be with you the whole day. I had a serious war going on in my head. I started thinking what about the rest of my life? Who can be in my head to calm thoughts down after the fact? The spirit of God was convicting me for the thoughts of abortion.

One day I was sitting on my bedroom floor and it was if God himself said if you go to the clinic you have already committed the abortion despite if you go through the process.

The rest is history. My baby was born. The abortion seed was canceled and the rest is still history. The devil wants to kill your seed because he knows the anointing and the power of God that flows through their loins is going to tear his kingdom down. You have to Ignore the devil.

You must press delete on those evil and wicked thoughts that he bring to you. Casting every imagination and every high thing that exalteth itself against the knowledge of God. You have to be open to hear the voice of God. Life is full of challenges and oppositions when you are dealing with people and involved in ministry. Whenever you are called there will always be things to divert your paths.

What you must realize is that being called does not make you an exception to crisis. In fact buckle up because collisions are about to take place. You must be geared up at all times.

Remember what Paul said in Ephesians, put on the whole amour of God so that you will be able to withstand the wiles of the devil. Being called automatically makes you a target for the enemy. Hold on! The mere fact that you are not just called but chosen the devil starts releasing his fiery darts at you, the target. See when you realize that you are chosen the whole outlook of your assignment changes. You now realize that your journey is not just about you but about those who are strategically assigned to you. Each and every person on this earth possesses a spiritual umbilical cord and there are people that are specifically designated to your cord. Their life merely depend on you. This is the reason why we must watch what we eat and drink.

Trapped in the System

When a person is pregnant they are no longer governed by their wants and desires but by the life that is connected to their umbilical cord.

Your appetite changes even the times in which you feed yourself changes. You are forced to put the right things into your temple because now even your health may depend on it. We must face it. We all are pregnant.

We have people tied to our umbilical cord and their lives and our very own depend on how we feed ourselves in order to sustain and give birth in a healthy way. We all at some point have had a spiritual abortion.

It may have been contributed to ignorance, laziness, selfishness, rebellion and many other things.

But it is time that we step up to the plate stand in a place of responsibility and accountability for our actions. God has given us everything we need that pertains to life and Godliness and there is nothing in this world that can overtake us.

We can no longer walk as babes. We must GROW UP!! You can no longer remain a grown child. Gear up!! Don't run from conflict Confront It!!! God has given you everything you need to confront the giant.

There are many things in life that we experience good and bad but our experiences are meant to encourage and strengthen us.

Do not, I repeat Do not let the storms of life tear you down. Put on your storm gear your HELMET OF SALVATION, your BREAST PLATE OF RIGHTEOUSNESS, your SHIELD OF FAITH, your FEET IS SHOD WITH THE PREPARATION OF THE GOSPEL OF PEACE, your LOINS ARE GIRD ABOUT WITH TRUTH AND have your SWORD OF THE SPIRIT WHICH IS THE WORD OF GOD!!

and declare that *YOU ARE A SURVIVOR!!! YOU ARE A THRIVER!!! YOU are Unstoppable, Undefeated and on the move!!!*

Chapter 4
Thought Patterns of Life

Thought patterns of life are contributed to what we feel in our spirit. You are what you eat. If you think you can do it you can. If you think you can't you can't. The bible says So a man thinketh so is he. Our actions are a result of our thoughts. We reap the results of all of the words that we speak. Life and death are in the power of what the tongue speaketh.(proverbs 18:21).

According to the book of James Chapter 3 our tongue sets the course of our life. Jesus speaks to the Pharisees about specific issues, but we must remember that the words of God govern our life. Words are powerful and the fruit thereof.

For out of the abundance of the heart the mouth speaketh, man shall give account on the day of judgment for every idle word that he spake.

For by thy words thou shalt be justified and acquitted. By your words you will be condemned and sentenced.

You must set the atmosphere for God to work on your behalf. He comes where he is invited and when he comes the atmosphere must be right. He works in the power of his word. Speak the word of God. Set the atmosphere so God can work in the power of his word. Speak and he will honor it. Yes he will honor it. Remember in St. Mark 11:23 part b says, he shall have whatsoever he saith.

Once again here we are reminded that there is power in your words.

Let's go down to Mark 11:24-25. It reminds us that the atmosphere must be right. Let's not limit ourselves of what and where the atmosphere can be. Here the scripture gives reference to the atmosphere of your heart, your inner man. When you stand praying Forgive, Forgive, Forgive. If ye have an aught against any that your Father also which is in heaven may forgive your trespasses.

Have you thought to yourself why is it so hard to forgive, Forget, Yes I said forget and let it go? Because satan and all of his evil forces knows that if your atmosphere stay cluttered there is no room for the King to come in. Unforgiveness along with the refusal to let it go keeps us stuck and hinders us from going forward to receive all that God has for us.

When we don't forgive and let it go, it forces us to a place of always keeping track of what, when, and where our offenders hurt us which makes it much more difficult for us to heal, forgive and let it go! Let it go! When you don't let it go you have allowed yourself, your mind to become a note pad that keeps records that becomes a diary of offenses. Let' take a look at this.

Diary of Offenses

Our mind is very complex. According to Wikipedia it states that the mind is manifested as combinations of thoughts, perceptions, memory, emotions, will and imaginations. It further more states that the mind is a stream of consciousness. It includes all of the brains conscious processes and thought processes of reasoning.

You see the mind is likened unto a computer. It acts as the hard drive. The mind stores all of life events in it. Just like a computer if the hard drive of your mind becomes cluttered with junk such as cookies and browsing history of visited places of offenses, it causes you to not function properly.

We must control our minds at all times. We can not I repeat we can not allow the cares of this world to cause us to miss destiny.

Destiny awaits you. Destiny is calling your name. Perhaps you can't hear her because you are stuck in a trance of where they last offended you. Get Over It!! I know it sounds harsh but you have an appointment with destiny and if you remain stuck you will miss the ultimate plan that God has for your life. How much more ground and time will you allow the enemy to continue to steal from you? Ok, let's talk. They hurt you. They offended you. They were wrong; you know it and they do too. Get Over it!! They stole your husband. They stole your wife. They scandalized your name and caused you to lose your job.

Get Over It! Don't allow it, them or whatever system that was used against you to continue to allow you to be stopped up.

Life is precious. It is full of divine opportunities. It is full of divine connections waiting for you to make your appointment. The table has been reserved and it has your name on it. They can't go to the next dimension of Kingdom because you possess the keys. The King has need of you. Your position of Royalty is awaiting your presence. The land need to hear your voice speaking to it. Walk in that wealthy place that God has called you to.

You are an eagle and there are certain things that eagles do. They confront the giant of the storm head on. Put on your storm gear and fight the good fight of faith. Eagles do not let the storm stagnate them or cause them to be offensive. But they use the storm as a propelling force to go higher.

They operate under great vision. They do not operate under the now but under far away visions of greatness. They look beyond what's on the horizon and soar as high as soaring can take them. We can't let the obstacles, challenges and situations of this life cause us to miss our destiny.

You must realize that it takes the bad as well as the good to propel us to the point of knowing that we have a brighter future of what destiny has prepared us. That is called greatness. Greatness is something that comes from within. It is birthed out of being made in the likeness and image of Christ. You have to walk in that place even when no one else is there to encourage you. You have to do like David and encourage yourself. You tell yourself I can make it. I will make it. I shall make it.

You must realize that because you have decided to read this book that you are in pursuit of greatness and everything you need to get through this is already in you. There is a King or a Queen living inside of you.

You are operating beyond belief but in inevitable faith knowing with an assurance that there is a word from the Lord for your life that is going to revolutionize everything that concerns you.

You are past belief. Belief is based upon the given results. The results say that you should have failed. The results say that you should have quit. The results say that you should have died before giving birth to your destiny. But faith says despite the results you pass. Faith says despite the results you live. Faith says despite the results you win. When faith is all you have just stand.

Stand against the wiles of the devil. Stand against the forces of darkness. Stand against the voices of negativity. When faith is all you have soar. Soar to the highest height using your storms as propelling boards. Soar like the eagles.

One of the oldest and wisest books declares in the book of Isaiah But those who wait for the Lord [who expect, look for, and hope in Him] shall change and renew their strength and power; they shall lift their wings and mount up [close to God] as eagles [mount up to the sun]; they shall run and not be weary, they shall walk and not faint or become tired.

Trapped in the System

You can no longer think and act like a chicken. You must now be the eagle that God has called you to be. E- is for extraordinary, A- is for ambitious, G- is for Great, L- is for longsuffering, E- is for experience in dependability.

You are now experienced in faithfulness, experienced in vision, experienced in discipline, experienced in commitment, experienced in determination, experienced in strength, experienced in integrity, experienced in courage, experienced in patience, persistence, and dedication. You have experience in single-mindedness, and of purpose. You have experience in allowing no circumstance, or obstacle or challenge to distract you. You are experienced in not letting your past impede on your future.

You now possess the characteristics of an eagle. When the trials and tribulations come again reflect back on the characteristics of an eagle and tell yourself I already have what it takes to get through this.

With a loud voice of triumph tell yourself I am built for this. Spread your wings abroad and allow them to take you in an updraft high above the turbulence that you are facing. Remember to ALWAYS seek GOD

Ms. Larita S. Rice

FIRST!! And nothing shall be impossible to those that have faith in God.

Poem by Larita S. Rice
Who am I?

Who am I? the person
deep down inside longs and
wonders who, what is this
person all about;

Screaming from the tunnels
of darkness wishing someone
hear my shout.

Uncover me I am smothering
Ahh a deep gasp, I am losing
my breath;

A massive loss of oxygen a
drastic change in my health.

Trapped in the System

I am a person that has been
hidden to the disguise of
others;

I am one who always lived
under the thoughts and
opinions of my Sistas and my
Brothas.

I am one whose wings were
crippled tied and broken;

I am one who didn't realize
that I was a designer's token.

Now...... who am I?

I am one who rose above my
circumstances on a platform
now I stand;

I am one who got my peace
prize, my new swag, walking

in my grown woman status
with my tall 6'6 man.

I am transformed through
metamorphosis my new
identity is top notch butterfly;

Ahhhh watch out, feel the
breeze of the cool midnight
waters…..
Ahhhh daylight hits
Up, up, up I now must soar to
the summer lit sky.

Chapter 5
Opposition From Within

In today's society we are faced with many kinds of situations we see on a day to day basis. Hunger, jealousy, envy strife, trouble in our family, mothers against daughters, fathers against sons, wives against husbands, lay members against preachers, governments against governments, countries against countries and self against self. You know it's a problem when you are against your own self.

Ms. Larita S. Rice

Growing up in the City of East St. Louis and the State of Illinois one can easily become consumed by its environment. The environment is such that it is encompassed by drugs, alcohol, gambling, prostitution and murder. The city has been in a destitute status for well over 40 years.

There has been many scandals and much corruption on a continuous basis. The local government positions has been filled with those who live, eat and sleep to operate with power and authority but not delivering sound results.

The city is amongst those recognized in the nation as poverty stricken and disenfranchised. Its population is mostly those who are uneducated, and unemployed. The way of living by many is made by the distribution of drugs. Simply because they feel trapped and can't see their way out. Many continued to live in the rat race of being controlled by politics and fear of politics is supreme because getting employment that may offer some type of security and benefits are controlled by those in authority and normally distributed to their family and friends.

The unfortunate thing is that it may not leave a whole lot of positions for others in or outside of the community.

I can attest to Solomon in the book of Ecclesiastes that life and the things thereof are connected to vanity. Living in East St. Louis makes it so easy for one to live in despair. It seems like everywhere you turn it is a dead end or do not enter. People who have acquired a little are selfish and are not really willing to share. It is as if they think that sharing of resources or knowledge limits them from sustaining or succeeding.

There is no reason to be afraid or intimidated when God's word has already said little becomes much when you place it in the master's hand. They live life with an attitude of I'm better than my fellow neighbor. It is hard to come up in an environment where all you see is dead ends and do not enters. This is why many live in despair.

They can't seem to see or find a way out. This has resulted in the involvement of illegal activity. People tend to most often turn to this type of activity as a result of stress, feeling trapped, feeling like a failure, a loser, less than or incompetent.

Isn't it something that the natural response to pressure is to fulfill the cravings of the flesh? This leads to drug abuse, sexual abuse, physical abuse, emotional abuse and so on. The people of East St. Louis have struggled a long time. We must remember what the scripture has said For we wrestle not against flesh and blood but against principalities in high places.

There are some strong holds over this city and they are closely related to extortion, prostitution, gambling and murder. A spirit of hopelessness and a serious I Don't Care Spirit.

Trapped in the System

When we are faced with so many strongholds it is easy for a city, a nation, or a generation to be overwhelmed and non productive. Many people, cities, and government bodies and so forth are dealing with strongholds, spirits of darkness, or curses and are not aware. In the area/city in which I live there have been dark spirits hovering over the city for years. These forces have ruled and reign for many decades.

Many tend to point the finger at individuals and say how corrupt they are but one of the main truths is that they are operating under curses and dark spirits and let's not forget that many sin because they are consumed with their own lusts, lust of the eye, lust of flesh and the pride of life. I remember growing up as a little girl seeing other families appear to be what we call successful.

They had big houses, fine cars and the apparel to go with it. I often wondered why my family couldn't or didn't have those things. I knew that they were smart and intelligent and possessed multiple skills.

I saw the struggles they had with paying bills, paying real estate taxes, transportation and making home repairs when needed. I grew up in a home that displayed some forms of violence such as verbal, mental, physical and emotional abuse.

Members of my family were and still are consumed with alcohol and drug abuse. This was passed down to me. I started drinking and smoking marijuana around the age12. Yes, I said 12. Well if you're wondering where my parents were my dad wasn't present and my mom was deeply involved in a relationship.

The relationship consumed her mind, body, soul and her time. She put a lot of time and effort in the relationship which pulled her away from me. The person whom she was involved with made fun of me and teased me because he knew I was hurting over this. He would display half smiles on his face as to say I got her and you don't. One day I got so upset I wrote too close for comfort on our kitchen cabinet and I got a whooping. The age of 12 was the beginning of my fiery trials.

My mom got so deep in this relationship that she began to do drugs. She became addicted to crack cocaine. She would neglect her motherly duties such as cooking, cleaning, and washing. My clothes would be dirty and my coat sleeves were filthy. I remember one day my aunt said girl you're old enough to wash your own clothes if your momma don't do it. That was a pivotal moment in my life where I was thrust into what we would consider adult responsibility. My life as I had previously known it would be changed forever. I was now growing up without a mother or a father.

I got my first boyfriend. We were together for about four years. He was also whom I lost my virginity to at age 12. He got off on drugs crack cocaine and some other drugs. He later became violent and started to beat me. One day I was at his house and he began craving the drugs really bad and I guess I was interrupting him. He began to argue with me. The yelling and screaming became louder and louder. His mom and sister who preferred his previous girlfriend over me and was somewhat scared of him never really interrupted the argument.

He began to grab me and it was getting violent. His mom and sister intervened. He snatched my shirt off and I ran out of the house onto a neighbors porch and hid. The boyfriend ran out of his house looking for me but couldn't find me. I tapped on the neighbors door and finally a guy answered how embarrassing. I am stripped to nothing but a bra and my bottoms. The neighbor gave me a shirt and he took me home. At this point of my life seeds of embarrassment, shame and fear were birthed in my life.

Somehow this wasn't the end. I lived and still do live a very compassionate life that has kept me bound to wrong relationships because I was unable to make good sound decisions. Just because you love people don't mean you can always help them or that you are called to stay. Staying in a place that God has ordained for you to leave ultimately brings destruction. It causes relationships to be broken some never to be restored and it interrupts the process of reconciliation. When we act as savior to those who have been assigned to our lives by God or by the devil we allow ourselves to enter into a place of depletion.

We must remember we are not called to fix people, complete people or change people. That is the role of the Father, Son and the Holy Spirit. I used to believe that was my role. I have discovered that we are compliments one to the other according to the assignment of the relationships. When we act accordingly there is a level of peace and comfort knowing that all things no matter what it looks like is working for our good.

There is always a constant war going on within us. Our mind is the battleground of good and evil. We have to constantly stay in the word of God so that our minds are renewed. We have to live our lives casting down every evil imagination, high thing, and corrupt seed that have been or trying to be planted in our lives. We must die to ourselves daily. Submit ourselves to the will of God. Walk in the spirit of God so that we don't fulfill the ill will of our flesh.

Trapped in the System

There is always a war going on in the flesh. Paul describes it in Romans chapter 7 as the war between good and evil. He says every time he would do good evil is present to deter him. He said For the good that I would I do not: but the evil which I would not, that I do. It is made evident in this passage of scriptures that there is opposition within. He says that now if I do that I should not, it is no more I that do it, but sin that dwelleth in me.

He describes the opposition of sin dwelling in our members that has grown and grown that our spirit man becomes overshadowed. He says For I delight in the law of God after the inward man: But I see another law in my members, warring against the law of my mind, and bringing me into captivity to the law of sin which is in my members. It was overwhelming for Paul to understand because everything within him wants to please God. But there are opposing forces that are pushing him to violate God's Law.

Paul says O wretched man that I am! who shall deliver me from the body of this death? Who shall cause me forward to the obedience to Christ. He says I thank God through Jesus Christ our Lord. So then with the mind I myself serve the law of God; but with the flesh the law of sin. Paul realized that we must die daily. He realized that unless we die to our flesh daily the flesh will control us. in Romans 8 Paul says For the law of the Spirit of life in Christ Jesus hath made me free from the law of sin and death.

[3]For what the law could not do, in that it was weak through the flesh, God sending his own Son in the likeness of sinful flesh, and for sin, condemned sin in the flesh:

That the righteousness of the law might be fulfilled in us, who walk not after the flesh, but after the Spirit.

For they that are after the flesh do mind the things of the flesh; but they that are after the Spirit the things of the Spirit.

For to be carnally minded is death; but to be spiritually minded is life and peace.

Because the carnal mind is enmity against God: for it is not subject to the law of God, neither indeed can be.

So then they that are in the flesh cannot please God.

How do we conquer this fight that goes on inside us? We must realize that our redemption and our power both come from the blood of Jesus. It is through the shed blood of Christ that we are redeemed from the law. What the law could not do Christ did. He has given us keys to the kingdom of God. His word declares we are to cast down, strip off, violently force off imaginations and thoughts that would work against the mind and the will of God.

We must study to show thyself approved so that when the enemy sends the powers of darkness to distract, deter, and divide you from the plans of God we can speak the word only. We can declare to the devil It is written. The Lord says that we have power to tread upon serpents. The Lord says the power of life and death is in our tongue. The Lord says that we are the salt of the earth. This is how we overcome the opposition from within by speaking the word only.

Confessing what God says for our life. We do this by reading the word so we will know what to speak to oppose the forces of darkness.

Chapter 6

At the Breaking Point

Breaking- to shatter by force, to weaken, violate, interrupt, to burst forth as a storm to change

Point- moment of time, purpose, to show direction or position by extending a finger.

At the Breaking Point

Sometimes we don't seem to understand the reason why we go through certain things. We can't seem to grasp that we must travel down the highways and by-ways of trials and tribulations. Often there are sometimes when the road becomes so dark that every time we move we are running into something. Sometimes our thinking becomes so cloudy that we just can't seem to surface it into clean air. In other words we can't seem to make sound decisions that are in correspondence with God's word. The pressure becomes so heavy that we feel pushed to make decisions that becomes life threatening, sending us down the road of destruction.

It is right here where it becomes so dimmed in our eyesight and so deaf in our ears that we don't see, hear or feel God anywhere or anyhow. We ask the question God Where are you? Why do you leave me alone to deal with this? Lord you said you wouldn't put more on me than I could bear.. We don't realize that the same God who dwells at the mountain top is the same God present in the valley. David declared in Psalms 39:8, if ascend up into heaven thou art there; if I make my bed in hell behold thou art there but because of the forces of the enemy we doubt the God of Abraham, Isaac, and Jacob whom we serve is awesome and omnipresent. Don't sell yourself short.

Pressure in the birth canal

Don't give yourself to the enemy for his purpose of hell, death and separation from God so that the destruction of your soul can be manifested. When at the breaking point the pressure is so intense. It is likened unto a woman in her final trimester of her pregnancy. The labor pains begin to kick in. The belly becomes so stretched and is very uncomfortable. Those things that used to accommodate her no longer do. The stomach begins to drop indicating that the baby is making its way even closer to the birthing canal.

The bladder gets the news that the baby is even closer to its arrival because it now responds to the level of the intensity of the pressure by preparing to release. Likewise in our lives pressure causes us to respond to the demands that it is sending. The question is how will we respond. Paul says in Corinthians 4:8-9 we are troubled on every side, yet not distressed; we are perplexed, but not in despair. Persecuted, but not forsaken cast down, but not destroyed. Even though these tough times come, it is an indication that delivery of the promise is almost here.

Ms. Larita S. Rice

Delivery is near

You can be certain delivery is near because the intensity of the pressure is great. We must hold on to the instruction of the word of God in 2 Corinthians 4 which says For which cause we faint not; but though our outward man perish, yet the inward man is renewed day by day. For our light affliction, which is but for a moment, worketh for us a far more exceeding and eternal weight of glory; while we look not at the things which are seen, but at the things which are not seen: for the things which are seen are temporal; but the things which are not seen are eternal.

Our perception determines our outcome of our situation. If I look at the glass as half empty then it begins to formulate a plan of self defeat as though progress is not taking place. But if I look at it as half full it begins to formulate a plan of yes I can. Although our trials and tribulation seems like they come to destroy us it is the way we choose to view them that determines how we will go through it. If we go through as a victim or a victor will determine our level of triumph and the flow of the benefits. God's word has declared that we are more than conquerors. We have to see ourselves as God sees us. He sees us through the blood of Jesus. God sees us through the atonement of our savior. We have to pray daily that our mind will become renewed so that we might think like Christ concerning our situations.

Chapter 7

The pain of sacrifice

As defined in the dictionary Sacrifice is to surrender for sake of obtaining some other advantage; anything given up for the sake of others. God never ask of us to give something that is not in our hand. The problem is that it just might be your ONLY. This brings me to the story of Abraham. Abraham was given the awesome task of being challenged for his only. The bible declares in Genesis the 22nd chapter And it came to pass after these things, that God did tempt Abraham, and said unto him, Abraham: and he said, Behold, here I am. And he said, Take now thy son, thine ONLY son Isaac, whom thou lovest, and get thee into the land of Moriah; and offer him there for a burnt offering upon one of the mountains which I will tell thee of. Here we have Abraham is not just commanded to give his ONLY son, but he is commanded to offer him up as a burnt offering. He was given direction on where to take his ONLY son to be offered up. Let's take a moment to imagine what Abraham may have been thinking.

We must remember some very important facts about this story. Abraham who was married to Sarah were both up in age. Abraham was one hundred and Sarah was ninety. When it was first prophesied to them about having a son they both laughed. They laughed because according to the clock of the body it no longer tick tocked the natural ability to bear a child. Despite what nature said the God who said let there be opened Sarah's womb and behold a son came forth.

Now let's take a deeper look inside. They both were old in age. They were beyond the natural ability for their bodies to bring forth a child But God. After they gave birth to a child despite what nature said, God says Abraham, O Abraham, I want you to give your son your ONLY son up for a burnt offering. Can you imagine how Abraham must have been feeling? This is the same person that in Genesis the 15 chapter had a conversation with

God about not having his own seed and the Lord even then said your heir will come out of your own bowels. God tells him look into the sky at the stars and will thou be able to number them so shall be thy seed. After all of this God opens the womb and says I want your ONLY son to be offered up for a sacrifice.

Abraham had to have some discomfort. Doubt had to have been knocking vigorously at the door of his faith. He had to have felt betrayed, let down, confused, uncertain of all the promises that had been made, But he pushed emotions aside and moved towards the obedience of God. The bible says he rose early in the morning to go to the place in which God had commanded. Despite what he may have felt like, what he might have been thinking, he moved according to what God had commanded. He didn't speak the circumstance he spoke Faith Only, God will provide a Sacrifice.

Abraham shows us in this passage the importance of having assistance to get to the place in which God has commanded. But once you get there you will only need the things in which God commanded you to have. Anything extra can be a distraction to the plan of God. He didn't even tell Isaac that he was the sacrifice to be offered. Let's imagine if he would have told Isaac, Isaac my ONLY son you are the sacrifice of the day. This could've, caused Abraham to disobey God. Let's imagine it was you and your child started asking where is the sacrifice and you said, you are the sacrifice and they began screaming and yelling and crying. What would you do? This is why it is important in those tough times of testing we don't converse with anyone but God. This alleviates all of the extra added distractions. What is your response when God ask you to do something? Do you respond immediately? Do you do what Abraham did pursue it early? We must act to the obedience of God despite how it looks or sounds.

We must not give God any old thing and think that it is acceptable. Do we respond in a way like Cain, I know I must offer up a sacrifice but it won't be my best. This is not acceptable to God. Then we are mad at God because we didn't get the promise. God only wants the best and sometimes that may be your ONLY.

A sacrifice is not a sacrifice unless you can feel it. We often times make deals with ourselves as to what a sacrifice is. We do this when it comes to giving offering, talents, time and our service. If whatever you are giving is not being felt by you chances are it's a gift and not a sacrifice. You see gifts come without a price. We give gifts all the time with no pain attached. Even the bible says gifts and callings are without repentance. We didn't get them because we endured pain. We received our gifts simply as a gift.

Sacrifice demands of us just as it did Abraham to give up something of great value. Even God himself gave his Only begotten son. God has required me many times to give my only. Even in my relationships God has required me to walk away from relationships that I thought was for a lifetime. He challenged me. It allowed me to know what place they were in my life. I was able to take inventory and make sure that my priorities were in order with God first, Family second and my working career third. God never requires anything of us that he himself has not already given. Remember the next time God is requiring you to give a sacrifice ask yourself can I feel some pain or discomfort in the sacrifice that I am giving? Do I feel stretched? and if you can answer yes to either one of the questions then you could indeed be rendering a sacrifice.

If you answer no to either one of the questions then reconsider whatever it is that you are giving. In all things through prayer and supplications seek God.

Chapter 8

Living out of the Hand of God

To live out of the hand of God is something extraordinarily magnificent. What better place to eat than out of the Master's hand. I can talk a little bit about living out of the Master's hand. I remember there were numerous times that I didn't have the money that I needed to take care of things that I needed to do. But the Lord provided me with favor in place of the money. There were times that I needed gas in my vehicle to get from a place and the Lord would lay it on someone's heart to bless me with money before I left or they would specifically say to me let me put some gas in your vehicle.

On other occasions we may have needed food in our house and I would get a call asking do you have food in your house and they would put money in my bank account so that I could buy some food. I'm talking about living out of the Master's hand. When you don't know where your next meal is coming from But God supernaturally shows up with manna from on high just as he did for the children of Israel providing them with food from on high. During our natural life here on earth many of us are exposed to different eateries and we develop different appetites. The problem is when we become hungry we will eat just about anything before us. Most times curving the hunger but it's not nourishing to the body. I'm sure you can relate to this.

Take a look. You're hungry, you go to the restaurant. The server comes out to take your order, because you're hungry you immediately decide you want appetizers along with any type of bread, crackers and cheese, soup or salad that you can get up front in addition to your entrée. The problem is because you're so hungry by the time your entrée arrives you have already filled yourself with junk and you have no room for the actual meal. Well in our lives this too applies. We live our lives with these bountiful appetites. We are hungry but not sure what we want. Let's not even go to what we need. We pick up so many things along the way. We develop bad habits. We form bad relationships and we refuse to detox and let it go.

That's right we need a good ole fashioned detox. One that cleanses to the core that can remove all those things that causes us to be clogged up. We need to remove all those things that causes us to have a fowl odor instead of being a sweet smelling savour. This brings me to a very familiar passage of scripture psalms 51. David knew that he had filled himself to the core with things that wasn't wholesome. He had ungodly desires and he cried out for God's help. He cried have mercy upon me O' God according to thy loving-kindness, according to the multitude of thy tender mercies blot out my transgressions, wash me thoroughly from my iniquities and cleanse me from my sins. David went on to say in vs. 3 for I acknowledge my transgressors and my sin is ever before me vs 10 says create in me a clean heart, O God and renew a right spirit within me.

You see the problem is that we never want to admit when we have done wrong. We eat the wrong things, we say the wrong things. We think the wrong way therefore we do the wrong things. It is not until we begin to take self-examination and admit to our wrong doing so that we are able to move forward.

Remember that the sacrifices of God are a broken spirit, a broken and contrite heart that our father God will not despise. God is eager to receive those who will trust him with every aspect of their life. He wants us to trust him to lead us, trust him to guide us, trust him to protect us and also trust him to feed us. The bible has already declared he that hunger and thirst after righteousness shall be filled. While you're hungry and not sure what you want, take sometime to feast off of the Master's table where the table is spread and the feast of the Lord is going on. You can't live off of natural bread alone but we live off of the very words that proceedeth from the mouth of God. It is very important to fill yourself with spiritual food because life and death lies in the power of the tongue and out of the abundance of the heart the mouth speaketh. Why not today choose to live from the Master's hand.

Pray this prayer with me.
Father today I choose to Live out of the Master's hand. I choose today to eat wholesome things that bring me life. Father I realize that natural bread alone will not sustain me against the wiles of the devil and that I need your word activated by faith which in return is a powerful force for victory. I speak life to every situation that concerns me. I speak life to every dry bone in my valley. In Jesus name I pray Amen!!

Chapter 9

Getting real with Yourself

Now that you have taken a step like David did and began to acknowledge your sins. Ask for forgiveness, repent and start moving forward so that God is at liberty to work. Remember at all times we must live a repentance life. David committed many sins and then he also took a long time to repent. Because David took a long time to repent his whole household suffered. The most ironic thing is that David is not alone. He like many of us who commit many sins are not taking the time to ask God for forgiveness and repent.

Somehow the enemy has us so blinded that we walk in shame and embarrassment before God reluctant of asking for forgiveness of our sins, iniquities, transgressions and trespasses. We somehow allow the embarrassment and condemnation to keep us from walking naked and not ashamed before the almighty God. We tend to forget that God is omnipotent, omnipresent and omniscient. He is the all knowing, all seeing ever present God. When we begin to live a life of transparency first with ourselves and then God it is then and only then can we experience true victory and freedom.

You see when we deny the fact that we are sinners yet saved by grace and that all our righteousness is as filthy rags then what we are saying is that we don't need a saviour and we start to think that we can change on our own outside of the word of God. You see you must understand that outside of God's word everything else is vanity. It is the word of God that shape, make and mold us. It is the word of God that causes man to come to repentance.

It is the nudging of the Holy spirit that woos us into accepting Christ and walking with him. The word cause our mind to be renewed and our desires to become God's desires. According to Romans 12, Paul pleads with us to be not conformed to this world but be transformed by the renewing of your mind. Transformation of one's mind can only take place except by eating, drinking, and sleeping with the word of God.

That's right you do remember in the book of Joshua chapter 1(kjv) verse 8 where it says this book of the law shall not depart out of thy mouth; but thou shalt meditate, that's right meditate therein day and night. There it goes eat, sleep and drink the word of God, that thou, that means you mayest observe to do according to all that is written therein: for then thou shalt make thy way prosperous, and then thou shalt have good success. Once again this comes from taking in the word of God. Your desires now becomes his desires and your way becomes prosperous because he is prosperous.

Ms. Larita S. Rice

We must realize that God has a plan for our lives. A plan to prosper us and give us an expected end. It is not until we come to ourselves that we are able to experience the true plan that God has for us. This reminds me of the story about the prodigal son. He decided that he no longer wanted to be at home and he wanted his father to give him his inheritance. He wanted to explore the world meet new people go new places. You know what it is like to feel trapped and feel like the boundaries are too tight. You want to break loose. The prodigal did just that he broke from the covenant of his family's inheritance. After getting out there and meeting new people and exploring new places life and the

freedom just didn't seem to be working. You see freedom for some individuals is not good when you are living under false perceptions. That is the perception of I can do what I want and when I want. The answer to that is yes you can. But remember that there are consequences when we make wrong choices. The prodigal son partied hard. He made friends and yes he did experience what the world had to offer that was to kill, steal and destroy everything that was originally designed by the father who is God. He discovered that everything while in the world is temporary. He began to live as an indigent and a misfortune rather than a child of the king.

He was living life in the manner that animals do. But one day he came to himself. When he came to himself he realized that he had wasted precious time and money. When he came to himself he realized that there was a better plan for his life. He realized that safety and provision was in the will of the father. He came to himself. We all like ships without a sail have drifted away from the original plan of our father. We are sidetracked and our true purpose is diverted. But when we come to ourselves and acknowledge our rightful position restoration can take place. God just like the prodigal son's father always stands with his arms open wide to receive us. We should always live a life where we are examining ourselves.

Examinations always shed light on things that need to be attended to in our lives. Perhaps you may be at a crossroad in your life and you may be wondering who are you? What's your purpose? How did you end up where you are at right now? First, let me tell you that you are royal priesthood, you are a chosen generation and you are joint heirs with Christ. You are created in the likeness and image of God. You were created to die to yourself that Christ may receive the glory through the sufferings and persecutions that we face and go through. Our Father has never and will never put more on us than we can bear. He always makes a way of escape for us. His plan is that he always may receive glory. Take a look. Do you remember the story of Lazarus? Jesus loved Lazarus and his sisters, Mary and Martha just as he loves you and I.

What is your purpose? I am so glad you asked.

Your purpose is to serve God with all of your might, all of your spirit, mind, body and soul. With every fiber of our being we are to become so submissive to God and his plan for your life that nothing else matters except your obedience to his call. Your purpose is to maximize your potential in every area of your life with full use and not slacking with any gift, any talent, and any skill that the Master above has given you. It is through these things that God gets the glory and you get the benefits.

Yes that's right your gifts make room for you and will cause you to go before great men. But there is something you must do to present your gifts and use them to make God happy. After all you were designed to live life to the fullest. Are you too guilty for not living life to the fullest? Me too. I was stagnated, wishy washy, doubled-minded and not moving consistently toward my destiny. It wasn't until I allowed God to wipe away the smoot of the fiery trials I had been in.

That's right you know life has a way if you let it of hitting you so hard. The fire can seem so hot that when you come out you are looking like smoke and smelling like smoke. But thanks be to God which gives us the victory in Christ Jesus. God says that it doesn't matter where you have been doesn't even matter where you are now, he purifies. He changes our garments and no one can tell where we have been but there is a clear and concise vision of where we are going and that we have been in the presence of God.

You know the old saying you see my glory but you don't know my story. God interrupts the story and adds I will give you a garment of praise for the spirit of heaviness. He interrupts and says I know the devil meant it for bad, but God makes it all good. Stand up fight the good fight of faith. You have been crowned for victory. Admit to God where you are. Let him fix you. Let him change your life forever. He has so many wonderful things with your name on them waiting for you to take hold of them. The sky is the limit.

Chapter 10

It's Time to get Connected

It's Time to Get Connected!

There are many things in life that come to distract us. There are things that are specifically set out by the enemy to destroy you. These things are to cause you to lose focus on the plan and purpose that God has for your life. They come in the form of **Dream Killers**. They get close enough to you to find out your plans and they do everything in your face and behind your back to cause the plans to fail. They are known as Delilah whether male or female coming in the form of an Angel of God only to be revealed as a camouflage of evil. They are known as ***Spiritual Abortionist.*** They are assigned by Satan himself to Kill your Baby in it's infancy stage. They want to get the umbilical cord all tangled up and zap the life out of your baby.

(But point to yourself and say The baby gotta come forth) Ahh Yea it's been ordained by God that the BABY MUST COME FORTH. The bible says in Romans chapter 8 **For whom he did foreknow, he also did predestinate to be conformed to the image of his Son, that he might be the firstborn among many brethren.** Moreover whom he did predestinate, them he also called: and whom he called, them he also justified: and whom he justified, them he also glorified.

Uhh when we talk about Jesus, we talk about our Redeemer, our Lord and Savior, he is **the Bread of Life**. He is also know as Jehovah Jireh.. Our Provider, **Jehovah-Tsidkenu, the Lord our Righteousness,** Yea he came that we might have life and that more abundantly.

Philippians chapter 2 says

Who, being in the form of God, thought it not robbery to be equal with God:

But made himself of no reputation, and took upon him the form of a servant, and was made in the likeness of men:

And being found in fashion as a man, he humbled himself, and became obedient unto death, even the death of the cross.

Wherefore God also hath highly exalted him, and given him a name which is above every name:

That at the name of Jesus every knee should bow, of [things] in heaven, and [things] in earth, and [things] under the earth;

And [that] every tongue should confess that Jesus Christ [is] Lord, to the glory of God the Father.

St. John 15:1-27(KJV) Provides another description of Jesus He says

I am the true vine, and my Father is the husbandman. 2 Every branch in me that beareth not fruit he taketh away: and every branch that beareth fruit, he purgeth it, that it may bring forth more fruit. Point to yourself and

Ms. Larita S. Rice

Say It's time to get connected. Maybe you have been living life under the leading of a person or a situation rather than under the auspices of the Holyghost.

Well, today is your day to get connected. Make a commitment that you will no longer look for other means of energy sources outside of God the Father. When we live life disconnected from the father we live life on life support of the world's system. It is your time and your season to thrust yourself into the things of God Strip off that spirit of heaviness and put on the garment of praise. Today is your day for a miracle.

Chapter 11
Processed for Change

In life we all experience some type of hardship, obstacle, disappointment or challenge. The bible says in 2 Corinthians 4 **[We are] troubled on every side, yet not distressed; [we are] perplexed, but not in despair;**

Persecuted, but not forsaken; cast down, but not destroyed;

Psalms 34:19

Many [are] the afflictions of the righteous: but the LORD delivereth him out of them all.

The bible reminds us that though we have many

Ms. Larita S. Rice

afflictions the Lord (look at yourself and say the Lord) UHUH the LORD, the Lord, the Lord…I know you thought it was your boyfriend, your girlfriend, your Job,

but the bible says the Lord delivers.. DELIVERS- to set free or liberate: *The Israelites were delivered from bondage.* DELIVERS- to release or save: *THE LORD DELIVERS THEM FROM THEM ALL.* **Although the pressures of life seem so hard and intense sometimes the Bible reminds us to** THINK IT NOT STRANGE concerning the fiery trial which is to try you, as though some strange thing happened unto you:

They are come to purify you, your trials and tribulations are coming to make you strong. (Point to yourself and say make me strong. UHUH. You see they are not come to make you weak, But they are come to make you STRONG.

They are like wheaties to your spirit they come to make you strong, they are building up your spiritual

muscles. They are causing your loins to be gird about with truth. David said *in Psalms 119:71*
[It is] good for me that I have been afflicted; that I might learn thy statutes.

My God, David! Are you trying to tell me that it was good that my boss lied on me? He says yes It was good for me that I had been afflicted.

Are you trying to tell me It was good that I went through that scandal? Yes, Yes, it was good for me that I had been afflicted.

Are you trying to say it was good that I was homeless for 11months with my 2 children with virtually no sound place to go?
YES, It was good. It was ALL Good, WHY? Because God is making you. He is processing you. He is allowing you to go through the refiners fire. He is purifying you. He's getting everything out that distorts your character. He's removing everybody and everything that hinders

you from your destiny. Behold the refiner shall come and when he comes he looks through the eyes of Jesus and says that's my daughter, that's my son, I have purpose for them, I have plans for you. Your destiny awaits you. I will purge you with hyssop. I will wash you and you shall be clean.

I will save you and you shall be saved. My God when the refiner comes he will sit on you.

I'm here to tell you that's why the pressure has been so hard UHUH. I am here to tell you, you are not about to die UHH MY GOD. You Shall live and declare the works of the Lord. You see the pressure is heavy because the refiner is sitting on you, he is forcing out everything that's not like him. Processed for change, you gotta go through some things. In order to reign with Christ we must suffer.

But after you have suffered a while the Lord will establish you and make you perfect, which means make you complete, nothing lacking, nothing wanting but whole in Christ Jesus.

Blessed [are] the poor in spirit: for theirs is the kingdom of heaven.

Blessed [are] they that mourn: for they shall be comforted.

Blessed [are] the meek: for they shall inherit the earth.

Blessed [are] they which do hunger and thirst after righteousness: for they shall be filled.

Blessed [are] the merciful: for they shall obtain mercy.

Blessed [are] the pure in heart: for they shall see God.

Blessed [are] the peacemakers: for they shall be called the children of God.

Blessed [are] they which are persecuted for righteousness' sake: for theirs is the kingdom of heaven.

Blessed are ye, when [men] shall revile you, and persecute [you], and shall say all manner of evil against you falsely, for my sake.

Rejoice, and be exceeding glad: for great [is] your reward in heaven: for so persecuted they the prophets which were before you.

Ms. Larita S. Rice

Psalms 1:1

Blessed [is] the man that walketh not in the counsel of the ungodly, nor standeth in the way of sinners, nor sitteth in the seat of the scornful.

But his delight is in the law of the Lord. Process … Processed for Change going through the channels for deliverance, developing new mindsets of God, forming Godly relationships that obey the principles of God.

to PROCESS means

a systematic series of actions directed to some end

the summons, mandate, or writ by which a defendant or thing is brought before court for litigation

to serve a process or summons on. (Point to yourself and say You just got served.)

There is a mandate from God upon your life. You

Will walk in greatness. You will answer the call of the almighty God to respond to destiny. I decree and declare that from this day forward nothing shall be impossible for you because you will operate in faith and the Kingdom authority that God has given you.

God bless you and may God keep you and may his face shine upon you.

Remember to constantly allow yourself to be ushered in the presence of God Seeking God first before making decisions and go rejoicing because the shackles have been loosed!!!

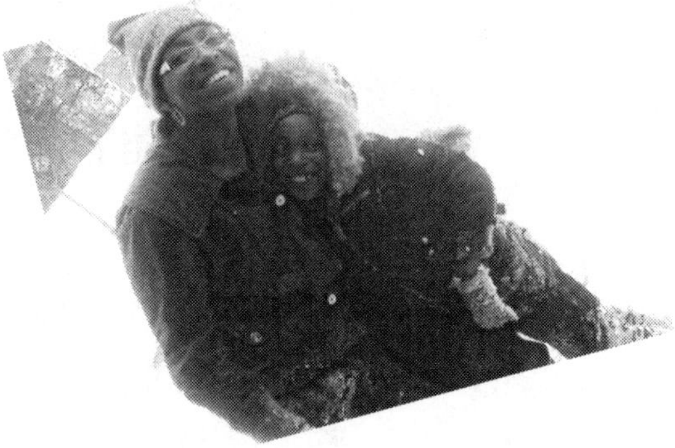

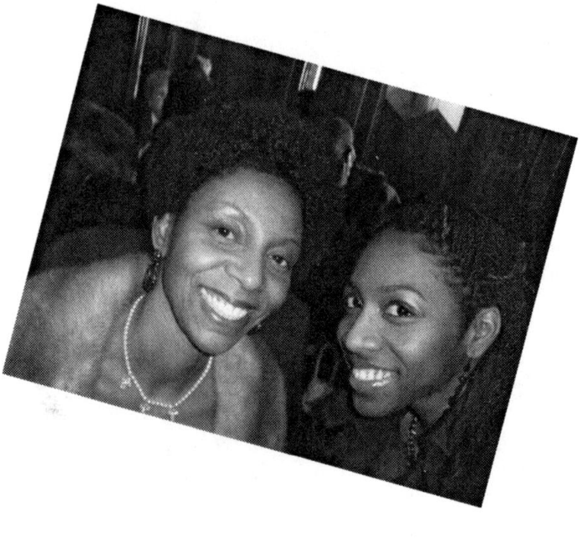

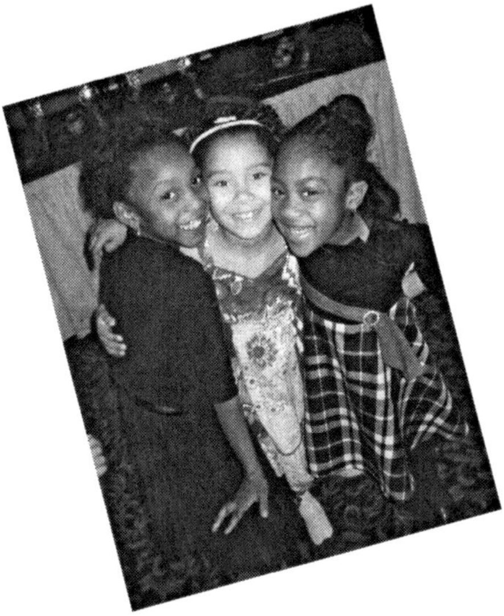

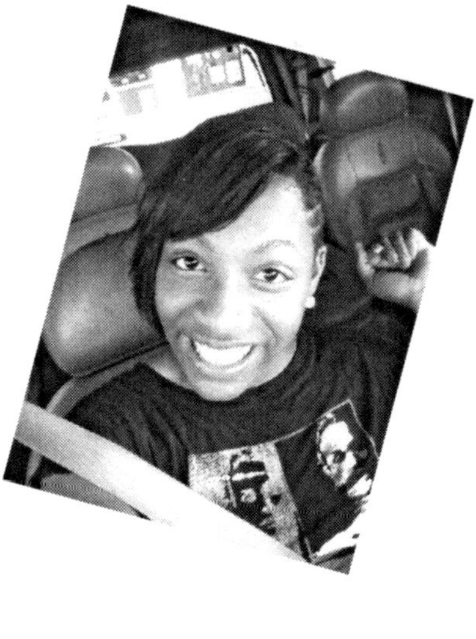

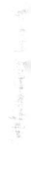

Book Resources

American Heritage Dictionary
Dictionary.com
http://www.earthlingcommunication.com/a/leadership/characteristics-great-leader.php

http://www.betternetworker.com/articles/view/personal-development/leadership/you-must-possess-the-seven-leadership-characteristics-of-an-eagle

Nike

Bible.com

Amplified Version

King James Version

Wikipedia